LAURA INGALLS WILDER

Activities Based on Research
from the Laura Ingalls Wilder Homes
and Museums

by Laurie Rozakis, Ph.D.

SCHOLASTIC
PROFESSIONAL BOOKS

NEW YORK • TORONTO • LONDON • AUCKLAND • SYDNEY

To Charles, age 12, and
Samantha, age 8,
who are setting off to blaze the frontier
of the 21st century.

ABOUT THE LEARNING CONNECTIONS SERIES

Learning Connections is a series of resource/activity books that Scholastic has developed in connection with museums, zoos, and educational institutions around the country. The series brings authenticity to educational materials by connecting teachers to the expertise and resources of these fine institutions. Learning Connections aims to extend the rich learning that occurs at these facilities to *all* students.

Scholastic Inc. grants teachers permission to photocopy the activity sheets from this book for classroom use. No other part of this publication may be reproduced in whole or part, or stored in a retrieval system, or transmitted in any form or by any means, electronic, mechanical, photocopying, recording or otherwise, without written permission of the publisher. For permission, write to Scholastic Professional Books, 730 Broadway, New York, NY 10003.

Book design by Sue Boria, Design Five
Cover design by Vincent Ceci
Cover illustration by Mona Mark
Interior illustrations by George Ulrich, Kathleen Watt
Photo reasearch by Donna Frankland

ISBN 0-590-49271-3

Copyright © 1993 by Laurie Rozakis.
All rights reserved.
Printed in the U.S.A.

Table of Contents

Introduction	5
Getting to Know Laura Ingalls Wilder	**7**
All About the Books	10
Westward, Ho!	**11**
Homesteading Mini-Book	13
Dear Diary	15
Prairie Schooner "Peek-Through"	17
Tracing the Ingalls Family's Route	19
State Identification Cards	20
Western Expansion and Native Americans	**25**
Frontier Food	**27**
Make Your Own Butter	28
What's Cooking?	29
Laura's Life in Town	**31**
A Prairie Plat	34
Make a Prairie Town: De Smet	35
Pioneer Paper Dolls	40
Community News	44
Buy This!	46
Reading, Writing, and 'Rithmetic	**47**
You Be the Teacher	49
A Lesson from Long Ago	50
Fun and Games	51
Writing the Little House Books	**53**
Family Portraits	55
Better Writing	56
Special Things	58
Special Places	59
Life Stories	60
Listening to the Past	62
Little House Country	**63**
Resources	64
Answers	64
Photo Credits	64

Introduction

When she was 65 years old, Missouri homemaker and poultry farmer Laura Ingalls Wilder began writing stories about her childhood on the frontier in the 1870s and 1880s. Her first book, *Little House in the Big Woods,* was published in 1932 and met with immediate acclaim. By the time Wilder had completed the eight volumes in her "Little House" series, 11 years later, she had become one of the most beloved children's writers of the 20th century, a standing that holds true today. More than 20 million copies of her books have been sold, and the books have been translated into more than 40 languages.

Why are Laura Ingalls Wilder's books so cherished? Reflecting on her youth on the rugged prairie, the writer once said, "It has been many years since I beat eggs with a fork or cleaned a kerosene lamp. Many things have changed since then, but the truths we learned from our parents and the principles they taught us are always true. They never change." Wilder's stories are both outstanding works of children's literature and invaluable historical accounts of the American frontier, and of an era in our nation's history that forever shaped the American consciousness.

This book grew out of my visit to the Laura Ingalls Wilder Home in Mansfield, Missouri, which houses a wealth of material I felt deserved a wider audience. An original manuscript, family photographs, artifacts, maps, diary excerpts, and newspaper accounts are all presented here to help introduce your students to the literary and historic dimensions of Wilder's work.

I wish to thank all the people at the museum who gave so generously of their time and expertise, most especially Connie Tidwell, Irene Lichty-LeCount, and Evelyn Underbakke.

Laurie Rozakis

GETTING TO KNOW LAURA INGALLS WILDER

(1867-1957)

In 1943, Laura's daughter Rose described her famous mother:

She's little, about five feet tall, has small hands and feet, and large violet blue eyes; I have seen them purple. Baby fine, pure white hair . . . . She holds a purpose or opinion like granite. She has a charming voice, with changing tones and colors in it, and is sometimes witty or fanciful, but this is always a little startling; she is never talkative and usually speaks in a matter-of-fact way. Often she is silent nearly all day long; she is completely self-reliant, is never lonely, has no need of companionship. She speaks only when she has something to say.

From *Laura Wilder of Mansfield* by William T. Anderson (The Laura Ingalls Wilder/Rose Lane Home Association, © 1982)

A Young Pioneer

The second child of Charles Philip and Caroline Lake Ingalls, Laura learned about the pioneer spirit practically before she could speak. Shortly after her second birthday, Pa, ever-restless for adventure and open spaces, decided to take his family on his trek west, leaving Pepin, Wisconsin, for Missouri.

After a brief stay in Missouri, the Ingalls family pushed farther west, to the Indian Territory of Kansas. Charles built a cabin on the prairie, but he and his family were unnerved by the Indians, who rightfully owned the land. The Ingalls returned to Wisconsin in 1871, but before long, Pa Ingalls loaded up the covered wagon and took the family west again, to the Minnesota prairies.

By 1874 they'd settled on the banks of Plum Creek, near the village of Walnut Grove, Minnesota. Charles hoped to prosper with a wheat crop, but a plague of grasshoppers hit the prairies, plunging the Ingalls into financial ruin. After a few years of grasshopper plagues, the Ingalls moved to Burr Oak, Iowa, and helped run a hotel. Laura and Mary waited on tables and cared for their baby sister to help their parents meet their mounting debts.

Continuing Hardship

When Laura was 10, the family returned to Walnut Grove. Finances were even tighter. Two years later, Mary was stricken with scarlet fever and lost her sight. Pa Ingalls became a storekeeper at a railroad camp in De Smet, Dakota Territory. During the family's second winter there, the settlement was struck by seven months of blizzards that made it impossible for trains carrying much-needed food and supplies to reach the area. Despite the fierce winter, the Ingalls clan survived. Pa and Ma Ingalls found time to instill in their children a love of books, and Pa often entertained his family in the evenings with fiddle-playing and storytelling.

To help her parents with the expense of sending Mary to the Iowa College for the Blind, Laura took a job teaching in a dreary, drafty schoolhouse 12 miles from home.

Married Life

When the school year ended in 1885, Laura returned home. Later that year, despite her misgivings about farming, she married a neighboring farmer, Almanzo Wilder. Her misgivings were prophetic, for within two years the young couple suffered crop failures, the death of their infant son, Almanzo's bout with diphtheria, which left him physically impaired, and the destruction of their home by fire. Only the birth of their daughter Rose in 1886 cheered their lives.

In desperation they set out for Westville, Florida, in 1890, but the torrid summers sapped Laura's spirits, so after two years, they returned to De Smet, South Dakota. They then moved to Mansfield, Missouri, and began farming at a place they named Rocky Ridge Farm. To supplement their income, Laura became a columnist for the *Missouri Ruralist*.

A Late Writing Career

Laura's daughter Rose Wilder Lane moved to San Francisco and became a well-known writer, often writing about her own upbringing on the family farm. She loved to hear her mother's stories about her pioneer days and encouraged her mother to put her childhood memories down on paper. Laura capitulated, figuring it was a good idea to save the stories Pa Ingalls told all those years ago. Rose edited Laura's manuscript and helped her find a publisher. Laura published her first book, *Little House in the Big Woods,* in 1932.

Soon after its publication, children from all over the country wrote letters begging for more stories of her rugged childhood. Laura acquiesced; in 1933, she published her second book, *Farmer Boy*, then followed it up with six more titles: *Little House on the Prairie* (1935), *On the Banks of Plum Creek* (1937), *By the Shores of Silver Lake* (1939), *The Long Winter* (1940), *Little Town on the Prairie* (1941), and *These Happy Golden Years* (1943).

Unchanged by Fame

Despite her popularity, Laura Ingalls Wilder's life changed little. When not writing, she continued to can the family's produce, tend the chickens, and cook the meals. After Almanzo's death in 1949, she stayed on the farm and attended local social events. She died at age 90.

All About the Books

Little House in the Big Woods, set in the 1860s, describes Laura's life as a young child in the Wisconsin woods. Mary, Laura, and Carrie are snug in the family's log cabin, sheltered from the wild winter winds. Pa supports his family by hunting, trapping, and farming. There is plenty of food and happiness. At night, Pa plays his fiddle and sings to his family.

Farmer Boy is the only book in the series that does not focus on the Ingalls Family. Rather, it chronicles Almanzo Wilder's childhood on a flourishing farm in Malone, New York.

Little House on the Prairie describes the Ingalls family's move from the Big Woods of Wisconsin to Kansas, then part of Indian Territory. The family is happy in their log cabin, but must relocate when the Osage Indians assert their rightful claim to the land.

On the Banks of Plum Creek finds the Ingalls clan in a sod house in Minnesota. Soon, Pa builds a house on the banks of Plum Creek, a venture financed on credit. Confident that he can pay his debts with the proceeds from his wheat harvest, Pa and the family settle into their new life. But just before the harvest, a plague of grasshoppers destroys the wheat and drives the Ingalls off the land.

By the Shores of Silver Lake picks up where the story left off in Plum Creek. Times are bad for the Ingalls family. They are deeply in debt and struggling to cope with Mary's blindness. In an effort to reverse the family's fortunes, Pa accepts a job in a railroad camp in De Smet, Dakota Territory. He sends for Ma and the girls, files a claim for a homestead, and builds a claim shanty. The book ends with the family living in the shanty.

The Long Winter recalls the brutal winter in De Smet, when blizzards halted food shipments. Many nearly starved, including the Ingalls family. Almanzo and his brother, Royal, help their townspeople when they find and distribute wheat that a farmer had saved for seed.

Little Town on the Prairie takes up the story of the Ingalls clan's life after the long, desperate winter. The people of De Smet celebrate their survival with social activities. To raise money to send Mary to a school for the blind, Laura works during the summer as a seamstress. Laura is courted by the dashing Almanzo Wilder.

These Happy Golden Years describes Laura's year as a teacher. Only 15, she is miserable in the drafty school house with her unwilling students, but endures for Mary's sake. The only bright spot is the arrival of Almanzo, who escorts her home every Friday to visit her family.

WESTWARD, HO!

At the end of the 18th century, the area west of the Mississippi River was a mystery to nearly all Americans. But in 1803, the West broke open. With one stroke of his pen, President Thomas Jefferson completed the Louisiana Purchase, opening up more than two million square miles and doubling the size of the United States. Eighty years later, 22 percent of the American people lived west of the Mississippi. Among them were the Ingalls family.

Cheap Land

Like thousands of other resourceful, independent people, the Ingalls family went west in search of land, livelihood, and living space. The Homestead Act of 1862 allowed a settler to acquire up to 160 acres of land by maintaining residency on the land for five years, improving it, and paying a registration fee of about $25. The lure of practically free land enticed settlers west, but homesteaders faced many hardships: harsh weather, plagues of insects, and limited availability of provisions.

The westward expansion of the railroads accelerated the settlement of the West. In 1869, the first transcontinental rail link was completed, and the West's open spaces became less remote. The American frontier soon passed into history and legend.

Student Activities

HOMESTEADING MINI-BOOK:

Students can find out some intriguing facts about homesteading and Laura's life on the frontier by making the question-and-answer booklet on pages 13–14. Make a double-sided photocopy of the pages and distribute a sheet to each student. To put the book together, have students follow these directions:

1. Begin with the side that shows panels A, B, C, and D facing up.

2. Cut the panels apart along the three solid lines.

3. Lay the panels on top of each other in alphabetical order, with the panel marked A on top.

4. Staple the book along the dashed line. Complete the booklet by folding it along this line.

Student Activities

DEAR DIARY:

On page 15 are excerpts from the diary of a woman whose family ventured west from New York to settle in Kansas in 1856. Distribute a copy of the page to students, and discuss the family's experience. Using the diary excerpt and the "Little House" books as reference materials, children can chart the positive and negative aspects of homesteading. You may want to provide children access to other books about pioneers as well (see Resources, page 64). Students can then pretend that they are young pioneers and write their own diary accounts of their experiences. As students write down their entries on page 16, encourage them to think about the work they'd need to do to set up a homestead, the difficulties they might face, the landscape they'd see, and the feelings they might have.

PRAIRIE SCHOONER "PEEK-THROUGH":

Pages 17–18 will help students investigate how the Ingalls clan traveled across the country. Make a double-sided photocopy of the page for each student. (Be careful not to invert the copy on the reverse side of the page.) After studying the various parts of the prairie schooner, students can hold the page up to the light to see what the Ingalls family carried with them across the country. Discuss with children differences between transportation today and in the late 19th century.

TRACING THE INGALLS FAMILY'S ROUTE:

Students can trace the Ingalls family's route across the country using the material on page 19. As an extension activity, students might enjoy working in groups to create an itinerary for a trip to the West today. How many miles could they cover daily in a car or camper? Where would they stop? How much would such a trip cost? (Students near the West Coast can plan a trip east!)

STATE IDENTIFICATION CARDS:

On pages 20–23 are cards that depict the states in which the Ingalls family lived. Divide students into pairs and provide each pair with a set of cards. Ask students to read the cards, then place them on a table, state side up. Students can then assemble the spinner on page 23 and play a game to identify the states by their shape. To play, have students take turns spinning and trying to find the state the spinner lands on. To see if they are right, students turn the card over. If their answer is correct, they can keep the card. If incorrect, the card is turned back over. The player with the most cards at the end of the game wins. Encourage students to create other games to play using the cards.

A

How fast could a homesteader travel?

When conditions were good, homesteaders like the Ingalls family could travel about 4 miles an hour. Usually, they covered no more than 15–20 miles in a 16-hour day.

B

Where was the land located?

The lack of water was the worst problem. Mosquitoes, stinging, wind-whipped sand on the plains, and a lack of heating and cooking fuel also troubled pioneers.

C

How much land could you get?

Pa Ingalls had to go to the land office with two witnesses to prove that he had lived on the land for five years, had built a house, and was farming 10 acres of land.

D

Who could be a homesteader?

Yes, if he had paid $1.25 an acre for his land.

What was the worst problem the Ingalls family and other pioneers faced as they traveled?

There was land available in all states except the original 13 as well as Maine, Vermont, West Virginia, Kentucky, Tennessee, and Texas.

How did Pa Ingalls prove his homestead claim?

A homesteader could get up to 160 acres of land.

Could Pa make his homestead claim in less time?

To be a homesteader, you had to be the head of a family, 21 years old, or an army veteran. Almanzo's sister, Eliza Jane, was a homesteader too.

The Ingalls family had a very hard time. How many families did not make their homestead claims?

Of the 400,000 families that homesteaded, two-thirds failed. They were driven off their claims after drought, grasshoppers, fire, hail, blizzards, and/or floods repeatedly destroyed their crops.

Homesteading West with the Ingalls Family

The Homestead Act of 1862 offered free land to people who were willing to help settle the West. The Ingalls family were among thousands of homesteaders who headed west in search of a piece of land and a new life.

Dear Diary (page one)

The Ingalls family was one of thousands of pioneering families who helped settle the West. This page shows passages from a diary kept by a pioneer named Miriam Davis Colt. In the spring of 1856, Mrs. Colt and her family left their home in New York and headed for Kansas. The Colt family went with a "settlement company," which was a large group of settlers. In her diary, Mrs. Colt writes about the hopes and disappointments of their trip.

January 15th, 1856 – We are making every necessary preparation for our journey, and our home in Kansas. My husband has sold his farm, purchased shares in the company, sent his money as directed... I am very busy in repairing all of our clothing... bringing everything into as small a compass as possible, so that we shall have no unnecessary baggage...

April 10th, 1856 – We are all in confusion – beds taken down, furniture sold that we do not want to carry, the rest boxed up... May Heaven grant that ours may be a prosperous journey...

May 13th, 1856 – Can anyone imagine our disappointment this morning, on learning from this and that member, that no mills have been built; that the directors [of the company], after receiving our money to build mills, have not fulfilled the trust reposed in them....

Now we all have come! Have brought our fathers, our mothers, and our little ones, and find no shelter sufficient to shield them from the furious prairie winds, and the terrific storms of the climate!

These intelligent, but too confiding, families have come from the North, East, South and West, to this farther West, to make pleasant homes; and now are determined to turn right about, start again on a journey – some know not where!

From *Went to Kansas* by Miriam Davis Colt (The Kansas Historical Society, © 1856)

Name _____

Dear Diary *(page two)*

Imagine you were homesteading in the 1800s like the Ingalls or the Colt family. Where would you go? What things might you see? What things might happen to you? Keep a diary of your homesteading adventure on this page.

October 1, 1882 _____

_____

_____

_____

November 15, 1882 _____

_____

_____

_____

December 21, 1882 _____

_____

_____

_____

February 1, 1883 _____

_____

_____

_____

March 6, 1883 _____

_____

_____

_____

_____

Name _____

Prairie Schooner "Peek-Through" *(page one)*

Many pioneers, including the Ingalls family, traveled west in a wagon called a *prairie schooner*: an ordinary farm wagon with a canvas top. The white canvas cover looked like the sails of *schooners*, sailing ships of the time. That's how the wagons got their name. After you take a look at the picture of the prairie schooner, hold it up to the light. What do you see?

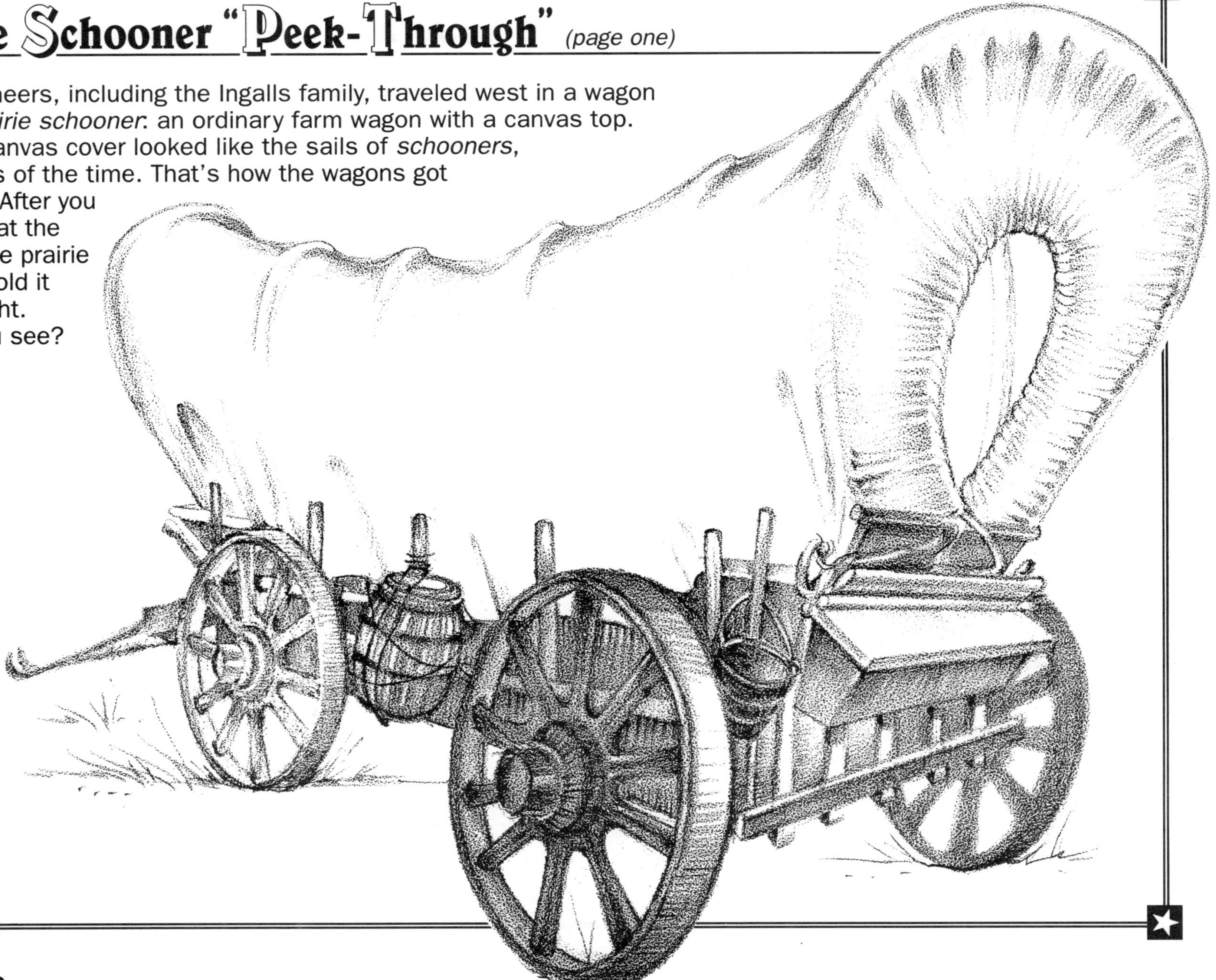

17

Prairie Schooner "Peek-Through" (page two)

See if you can find all the things Laura's family carried across the country in their prairie schooner:

- a "spider" (three-legged frying pan)
- a hatchet
- Pa's fiddle
- a barrel of molasses
- Laura's rag doll
- quilts
- a sack of white flour
- bundles of dried herbs
- a tin washbasin
- clothing
- a washtub
- a rifle and a bullet pouch
- a coffee mill
- a barrel of salt pork
- sacks of seeds
- a trunk
- a tin cup

Pack Your Bags:
Pretend you are going homesteading. The wagon is almost packed—there's just enough room for ten of your things. What would you take?

18

Name

Tracing the Ingalls Family's Route

The Ingalls family was always on the move! Here is a chronological list of most of the places they lived. Use this list to trace their route across the country on the map.

1. Pepin, Wisconsin (*Little House in the Big Woods* was set here.)
2. Independence, Kansas (*Little House on the Prairie* was set here.)
3. Pepin, Wisconsin
4. Walnut Grove, Minnesota (*On the Banks of Plum Creek* was set here.)
5. Burr Oak, Iowa
6. Walnut Grove, Minnesota
7. De Smet, South Dakota (*By the Shores of the Silver, The Long Winter, Little Town on the Prairie,* and *These Happy Golden Years* were all set here.)
8. Mansfield, Missouri

State Identification Cards

The state identification cards on these four pages will help you learn more about the places Laura and her family lived. To make the cards, cut along the solid lines. Then tape or paste together the front and back of each card.

Iowa

Statehood: 1846; 29th state
Capital: Des Moines
1870 population: 1,194,020
1990 population: 2,913,808
Book Set There: None. Iowa is the only place Laura lived during her childhood that she doesn't write about in the "Little House" books.
Wilder Fact: Laura's family moved to Burr Oak, Iowa, from Minnesota in 1876. They stayed there for just one year. While in Iowa, the Ingalls clan helped run a hotel. But Burr Oak was an old, settled town, and Pa was restless there. It wasn't long before they were back in their covered wagon, heading west.

Kansas

Statehood: 1861; 34th state
Capital: Topeka
1870 population: 364,399
1990 population: 2,364,236
Book Set There: *Little House on the Prairie*
Wilder Fact: When the Ingalls family moved to Kansas in 1869, they unknowingly built their house on what was rightfully Indian land. At night, the Native Americans held meetings to decide whether or not they should drive the settlers away. Laura's strongest memories of Kansas were of the Indians' pounding drums and loud chants. But she also remembered the peaceful side of the southern Kansas prairie—the endless blowing grasses and the enormous sky that surrounded her family's little house.

State Identification Cards

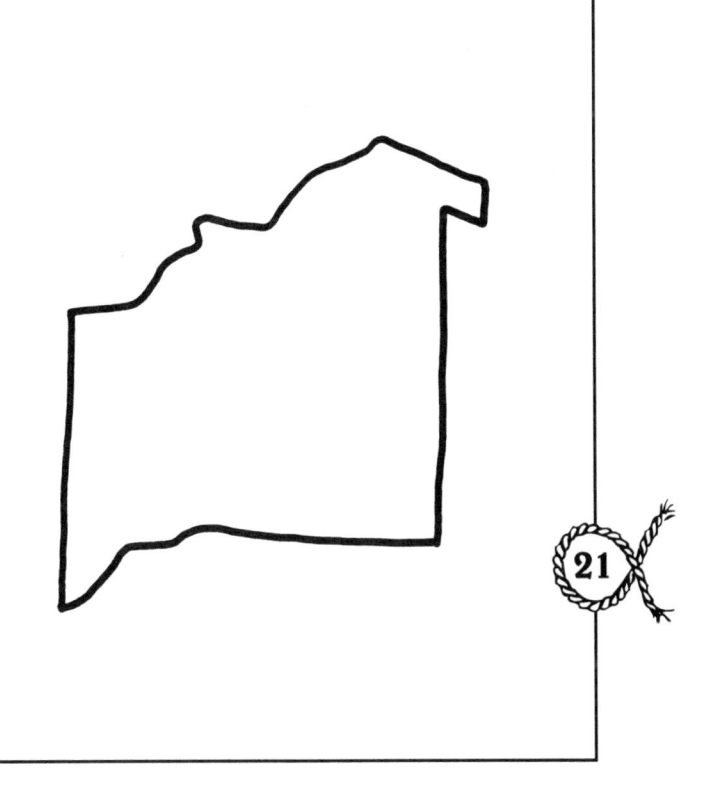

Minnesota

Statehood: 1858; 32nd state
Capital: St. Paul
1870 population: 439,706
1990 population: 4,075,970
Book Set There: *On the Banks of Plum Creek*
Wilder Fact: The Ingalls family first moved to Minnesota in 1874. At first they lived in a sod, or soil, house. Pa then built a home out of wood, planning to pay for it with the proceeds from his wheat crop. But just before the harvest, swarms of grasshoppers dropped out of the sky like hail and ate up all the crops for miles around. His crops ruined, Pa decided to leave what he called such "blasted country."

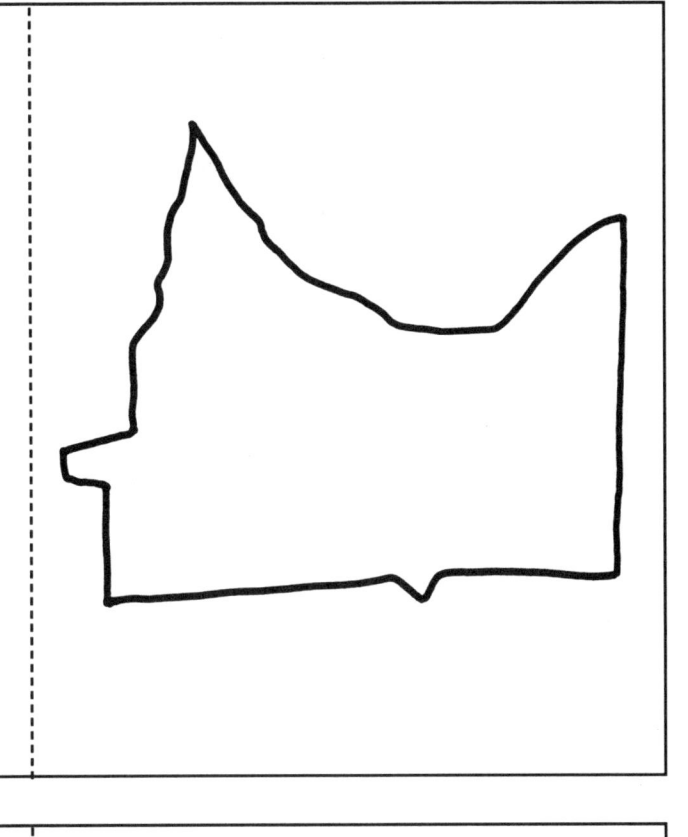

Missouri

Statehood: 1821; 24th state
Capital: Jefferson City
1870 population: 827,922
1990 population: 4,916,766
Book Set There: *All the Way Home: A Diary of a Trip from South Dakota to Mansfield, Missouri*
Wilder Fact: In 1894, Laura set out for the last time in a covered wagon to search for a new home. After living on the flat, treeless prairie, Laura longed for different scenery. She found it in the rolling, wooded hills of the Ozark Mountain country in Mansfield, Missouri. Laura and Almanzo spent the rest of their lives in Mansfield. It was there that Laura wrote the "Little House" books.

State Identification Cards

New York

Statehood: 1788; 11th state
Capital: Albany
1850 population: 3,097,000
1990 population: 17,950,000
Book Set There: *Farmer Boy*
Wilder Fact: Laura's husband, Almanzo James Wilder, was born near Malone, New York, on February 13, 1857. Laura never saw Malone or the farm on which Almanzo grew up. She depended completely on her husband's memory to write *Farmer Boy*, which is about Almanzo's childhood. It is the only book in the "Little House" series that is not about Laura and her family.

South Dakota

Statehood: 1889; 40th state
Capital: Pierre
1870 population in Dakota Territory: 11,776
1990 population: 690,768
Books Set There: *By the Shores of Silver Lake; The Long Winter; Little Town on the Prairie; Those Happy Golden Years;* and *The First Four Years*
Wilder Fact: The Ingalls family made South Dakota their final stopping place, and it was Laura's home from 1879-1894. During one Dakota winter, the Ingalls clan and other settlers barely survived howling blizzards that buried the prairie in snow. It was in De Smet that Laura met her future husband, Almanzo Wilder, whom she married on August 25, 1885, when she was 18 years old.

22

State Identification Cards

Wisconsin

Statehood: 1848; 30th state
Capital: Madison
1870 population: 1,054,670
1990 population: 4,705,642
Book Set There: *Little House in the Big Woods*
Wilder Fact: On February 7, 1867, Laura Elizabeth Ingalls was born in Pepin, Wisconsin. Laura's earliest memories in life were of her family's cozy log house and the great, dark trees of the Big Woods around them. In 1869, the Ingalls family left Wisconsin because Pa felt the Big Woods were becoming too crowded. In 1850, there were 305,400 people in Wisconsin; by 1870 the population was more than a million!

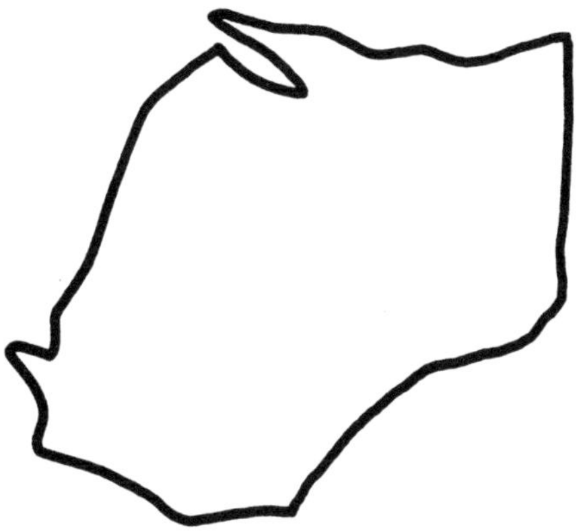

To assemble the spinner:

Cut out the spinner. Poke a brass fastener into the middle of the spinner. Open up a paper clip to make an "S" shape. Attach the paper clip to the brass fastener, as shown.

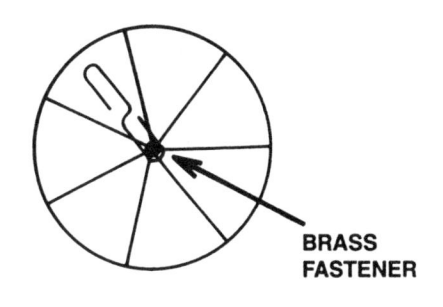

BRASS FASTENER

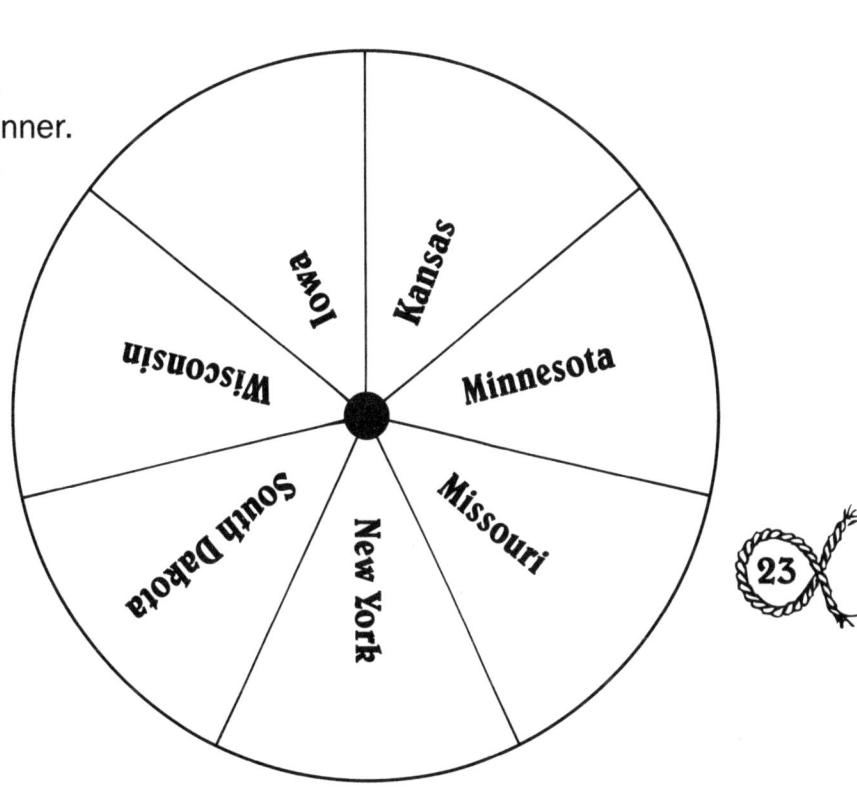

Spinner sections: Iowa, Kansas, Minnesota, Missouri, New York, South Dakota, Wisconsin

23

WESTWARD EXPANSION AND NATIVE AMERICANS

Americans who moved west in the 1800s saw it as an opportunity to improve their lives. With the Homestead Act of 1862, anyone willing to cope with the rigors of the unsettled West could acquire beautiful, open land for free. But the relentless westward expansion was a disaster for Native Americans. The U.S. government viewed Indians as an impediment to western expansion. The 1830 Indian Removal Bill, which authorized removal of eastern tribes to places west of the Mississippi, further bolstered the "rights" of settlers to dispossess Native Americans wherever they found them—even in regions west of the Mississippi. Some tribes, notably the Comanches, Apaches, and Sioux, tried to resist the unjust invasion of settlers by battling U.S. cavalry.

Fear and Distrust

In *Little House on the Prairie,* Laura describes her family's numerous encounters with the Plains Indian tribes. The Ingalls clan, as well as the other settlers in that remote corner of Kansas, feared and distrusted the Plains Indians. Ma disliked Indians, but Pa found them to be peaceable—when not provoked by settlers.

Loss of Land

Although the Plains Indian tribes were successful in driving early settlers like the Ingalls out of Kansas, theirs was a brief victory. By 1890, no Indian titles to land remained and the Native American population had been largely restricted to reservations or inferior land. (See page 26 for a map that shows the shrinking Native American land.)

Student Activities

A DIFFERENT POINT OF VIEW:

Ask students to find passages in the "Little House" books that describe the settlers' perceptions of Indians and encounters with them. Discuss with children why settlers felt the way they did. Then ask children to consider westward expansion from the Native Americans' point of view. Discuss why Native Americans might have been hostile toward settlers. For example, the settlers' encroached on Indian land, the U.S. government broke treaties, and the settlers unwittingly exposed Indians to devastating diseases such as small pox.

Student Activities

Divide students into groups. Have each group research how the flood of settlers threatened the way of life of a Plains Indian tribe, such as the Sioux, Crow, Comanche, Cheyenne, or Arapaho. Have groups present their findings to the class.

PEACE TALKS:

During the 1800s, U.S. government representatives periodically held peace councils with tribal leaders to try to negotiate land rights. After students conduct their research in the activity above, hold a class peace council. Students can role play government officials and Indian chiefs to present both sides of the land-ownership issue.

NATIVE AMERICAN LAND:

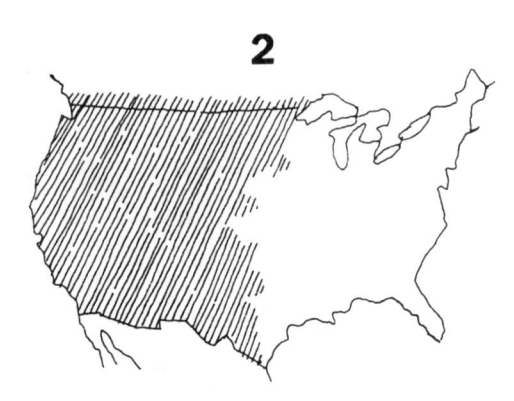

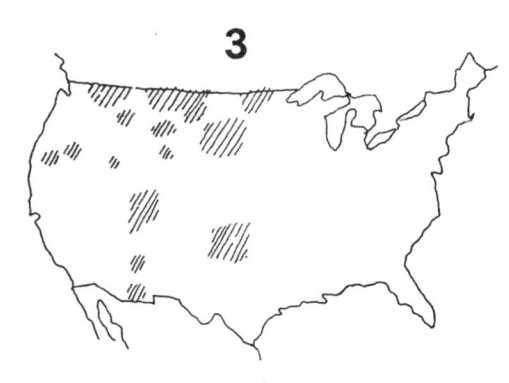

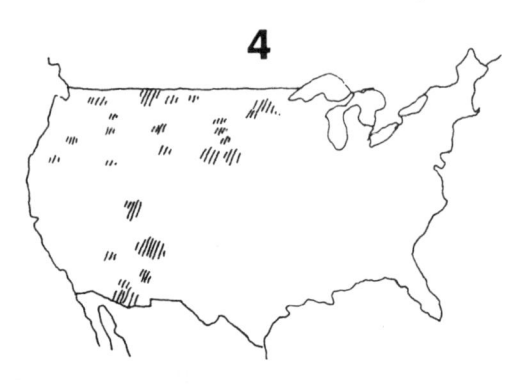

Native American land

1. Native American land before the arrival of the white man
2. Native American land, 1850
3. Reservations, 1875
4. Reservations today

FRONTIER FOOD

Families on the frontier devoted a great deal of time and energy to gathering, preparing, and storing food. Laura Ingalls Wilder's books reflect this aspect of pioneer life; much of her prose focuses on how the settlers hunted animals, and grew, cooked, and preserved vegetables.

Laura's stories also detail how geography and weather dictated the kinds of foods that were eaten, as well as the abundance or paucity of food. In the Big Woods, for example, settlers ate roasted bear and deer; on the prairie, jack rabbits and prairie hens wound up on the dinner plate.

No Fast Food

Laura and her family—along with other settlers—worked hard for their meals. Without butchers, farmers had to butcher their own pigs and other livestock, pluck game, and clean fish. They milked cows, made their own bread, and tended the garden. Unless you had an icehouse, there was no refrigeration. Foods were salted, dried, or stored in the natural freezer—outside.

Garden Treats

Laura thought that fresh vegetables were special and wonderful, because they were so hard to come by on the prairie. Without a garden, there was no crispy lettuce, tasty peas, or succulent green beans. When possible, the Ingalls family stored carrots, cabbages, potatoes, turnips, pumpkins, and squash in their root cellar.

Many of the fruits and vegetables we eat today—like Delicious apples and iceberg lettuce—did not exist in Laura's day, and others—like potatoes and corn—were very different.

Student Activities

MAKE YOUR OWN BUTTER:

By following the instructions on page 28, students can make butter by a process similar to the one Laura's family used. Divide children into groups of six, and provide each group with a copy of the recipe and the materials listed. Remind students to work with clean hands and utensils.

WHAT'S COOKING?

On pages 29–30 is a cut-and-paste activity that will familiarize students with some common frontier foods. Make copies of both pages and distribute a set to each child. Tell students to cut along the solid lines, then glue the two pages together along the edges only. That way, they'll be able to lift the flaps on the top page after the glue has dried.

Make Your Own Butter

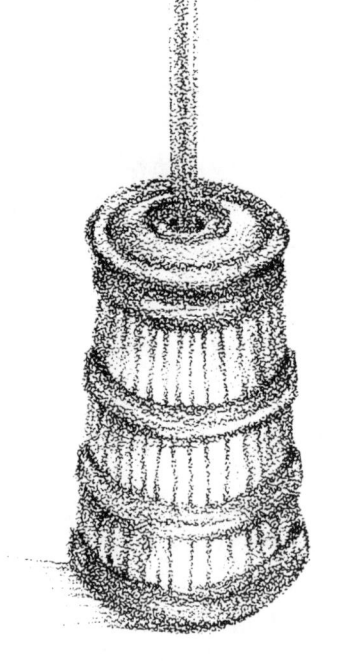

In Laura's day, there were no supermarkets at which to buy food. People prepared just about everything they ate themselves. On pages 29-33 of *Little House in the Big Woods*, Laura describes how Ma made butter. Here's how you can make butter.

You Will Need:

- 1 pint of heavy cream
- a large glass jar with a tight lid
- cup
- spoon
- strainer
- running water
- salt
- plastic knife
- crackers

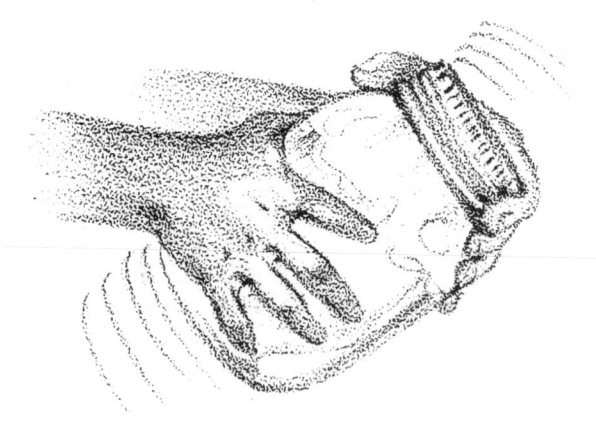

1. Pour the pint of heavy cream into the jar. Screw on the lid tightly.

2. Working with your partners, take turns shaking the jar until you see bits of butter. This will take at least 15 minutes.

3. Refrigerate the jar for an hour.

4. Pour the contents of your jar into a strainer, holding the strainer over a sink.

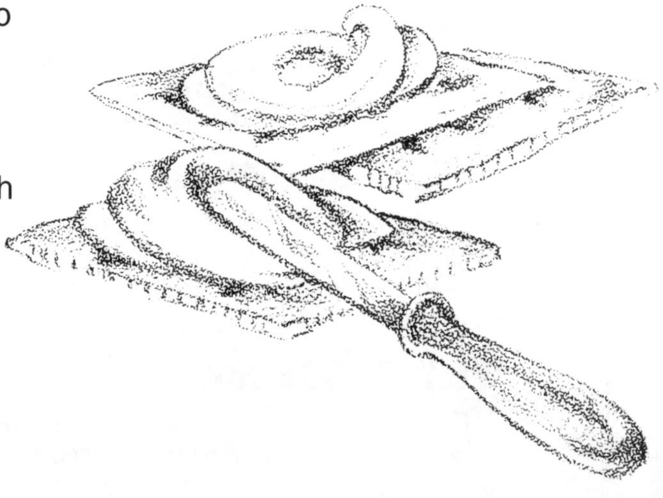

5. Take turns rinsing the butter with cold, clean water until it firms up. Spoon the butter into a small cup. Add a little salt, if you wish.

6. Spread the butter onto crackers and enjoy!

What's Cooking? *(page one)*

For frontier settlers, what they ate depended on where they lived. Settlers hunted, trapped, gathered, and grew just about all of their own food.

What did the Ingalls family eat? Cut along the solid lines of the three stove doors and four pot lids on this page. Then glue this page to the next page. When the glue is dry, fold back the flaps to see some of Laura's favorite foods.

What's Cooking? *(page two)*

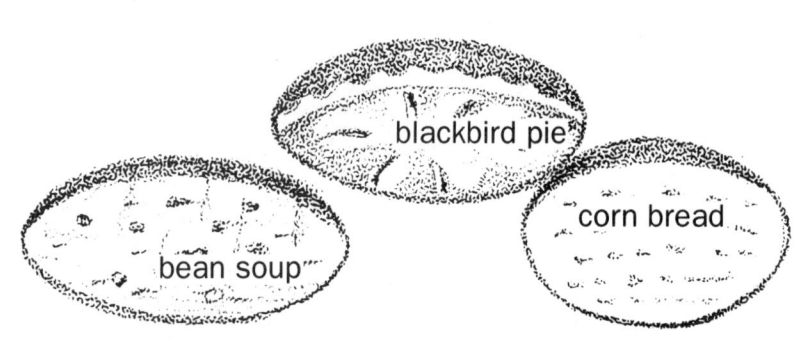

blackbird pie

stewed jack rabbit

bean soup

corn bread

pig's tail

roasted bear

bread

LAURA'S LIFE IN TOWN

During the summer of 1879, the westward-forging Chicago and Northwestern railroads set up a construction camp on the north side of Silver Lake, a mile east of De Smet, Dakota Territory. It was an untamed area, where herds of antelope still thundered across the prairie, spooked by the howls of coyotes. The Ingalls clan was the first family to move to the area.

A Town Begins

Later in 1879, two brothers, Almanzo and Royal Wilder, and their sister, Eliza Jane, filed homesteads to the north and west of De Smet. A newspaper set up shop a year later. Pa Ingalls recorded the beginnings of the community in a four-page piece he called "The Settlement of De Smet." Here is an excerpt:

It was about the first of March that I built a house on the townsite, and a man named Beardsley commenced to build a hotel about the same time, and E.M. Harthorn began erection of a store a few days later. V.V. Barnes came about March 12, with lumber for a claim shanty on his claim a half mile west of De Smet. He went to bed there with a thermometer beside him and when he arose it showed 12 degrees below zero.

From *On the Way Home* by Laura Ingalls Wilder (HarperCollins, 1992)

Pa's account ends with the report that 16 buildings and a railroad depot were being built on the townsite in the summer of 1880. Laura drew from this account for *Little Town on the Prairie*.

Student Activities

A PRAIRIE PLAT:

Students can develop their map-reading skills as they examine an actual hand-drawn plat made by Laura that appears on page 34. The plat depicts the town of De Smet—the setting for the last five books in the "Little House" series—as Laura remembers it. You can then guide children to make their own neighborhood plats using Laura's drawing as a model.

MAKE A PRAIRIE TOWN: DE SMET:

On pages 35-39, you will find drawings of De Smet's buildings in the 1880s. Laura described each of these buildings in her books. Provide groups of children with photocopies of these pages and have them work together to construct the buildings. After the houses are assembled, children can reread *Little Town on the Prairie* and create a bulletin board depicting De Smet as Laura described it. Students may want to paint or draw a background for the buildings.

PIONEER PAPER DOLLS:

On pages 40-43 are cut-out figures of a pioneer girl, boy, woman, and man and their clothing. Distribute photocopies of these pages to students. Students might enjoy using the figures with the bulletin board display they constructed in the activity above, reenacting scenes from the "Little House" books set in De Smet (*By the Shores of Silver Lake, The Long Winter, Little Town on the Prairie, Those Happy Golden Years,* and *The First Four Years*).

COMMUNITY NEWS:

A photograph and excerpts from an 1886 copy of the *Kingsbury County News*—a newspaper serving De Smet—appear on pages 44-45. Because there were few telephones in rural communities in those days, Laura and her family often learned what other townspeople were doing by reading announcements about them in the newspaper. Distribute photocopies of these pages to groups of students. Groups can read and discuss the announcements that appeared in the *Kingsbury County News,* then use the second page of the reproducible to create a community newspaper of their own. When everyone is finished, you might want make photocopies of each group's newspaper to share with the rest of the class.

BUY THIS!:

On page 46 are some advertisements culled from the same 1886 copy of the *Kingsbury County News*. Since there was no radio or television during Laura's childhood, the newspaper was one of the best ways for people to

Rose

From left to right: Ma, Carrie

A Family

Laura moved often and lived in many different houses during her childhood. But for Laura, home wasn't really a place. It was the people around her: Pa, her sisters, Almanzo. Here are photographs of Laura and the people who meant home to her.

ura, Pa, Grace, and Mary

Album

Laura and Almanzo

Pa and Ma

Student Activities

promote their businesses. Distribute a photocopy to each student. Discuss the ads with your class, asking questions such as: How are these ads similar to ones you'd see today? How are they different? What things are around today that weren't around in Laura's day? Then challenge students to create "old-fashioned" ads of their own. Before they begin, encourage them to use the "Little House" books to research items that might be sold in a pioneer town like De Smet. When everyone is done, share the ads with the entire class.

LOOKING BACK:

The last five books in the "Little House" series record the settlement of the town of De Smet, South Dakota. Children may enjoy researching the history of their own town or city. Students can visit the town hall, local library, and some of the older buildings in your area to begin their research. Local newspaper archives are also excellent sources of information. Students may want to conduct interviews with older residents in your community to gather information as well. Some questions to research:
When was the town founded and by whom?
What were the first businesses?
Who were some of the prominent figures in the community?
What was the character of the town? How has it changed?

Name _____

A Prairie Plat

A "plat" is a map or plan of an area. Here is a plat that Laura made that shows what De Smet, South Dakota, looked like in 1888. Laura drew the map to help her remember the town more clearly as she wrote some of the books in the "Little House" series. Use the map to answer the questions.

1. What street is Cap Garland's house on? _____
2. Are the railroad tracks north or south of town? _____
3. Is the school building east or west of Pa's house? _____
4. Which hotel is next to Harthorn's grocery store? _____

Draw Your Own Plat: Laura drew her plat by trying to picture her old hometown in her mind. Think of an area in your town or city. You might want to pick a few blocks in the center of town. Try to picture the area in your head. Think of the buildings, street names, and other landmarks. Now draw a plat of this area on the back of this page from memory, just as Laura did.

Make a Prairie Town: De Smet (page one)

You can recreate the frontier town of De Smet. To make the buildings, cut on the solid lines and fold on the dashed lines. Then glue the outside of the building over the inside of the building. Lift the flaps to open the doors and windows.

Beardsley's Hotel

Beardsley's hotel provided room and board (food) for folks new to De Smet or just passing through. Carrie Ingalls was a good friend of Mamie Beardsley, the owners' daughter.

Make a Prairie Town: De Smet *(page two)*

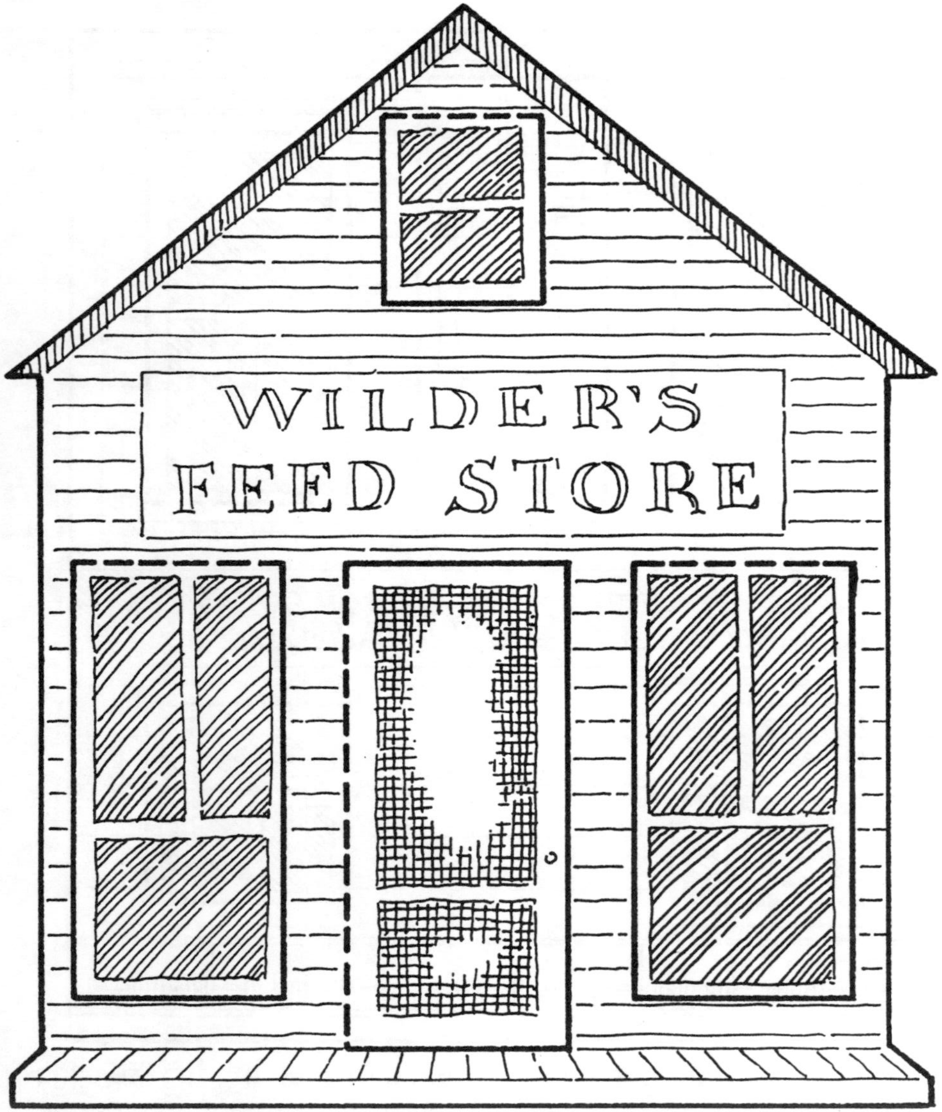

Wilder's Feed Store

Royal and Almanzo Wilder ran the feed store in addition to homesteading on their claim outside town. The two bachelors lived snugly there during the blizzards of the hard winter of 1881.

Make a Prairie Town: De Smet *(page three)*

Clancy's Dry Goods

To help raise money to send Mary to school, Laura sewed buttonholes on shirts sold at Clancy's Dry Goods. For six weeks of work, she earned $9. One dollar in 1880 would equal $8 in the 1990s.

37

Make a Prairie Town: De Smet (page four)

Surveyor's House

Laura and her family were invited to live in the Surveyor's house during their first winter in town. In 1880, the house became a hotel for the "spring rush" of homesteaders passing through the area on their way west. The Ingalls family charged 25 cents for a meal and 25 cents for a place to sleep.

Make a Prairie Town: De Smet (page five)

Schoolhouse

Laura and Carrie went to a one-room schoolhouse in De Smet. It was there that Laura learned her lessons so that she could become a teacher. She received her teaching certificate when she was only 15!

39

Pioneer Paper Dolls: Girl (page one)

Laura, Mary, and Ma sewed almost all of the family's clothes by hand until Pa surprised Ma with a sewing machine in *These Happy Golden Years*. Laura and her family wore clothes like the ones you will see on these pages.

Country girls like Laura usually wore dresses made from calico (cotton printed with small flowers). Sometimes their dresses were lined with canvas for extra warmth. They never wore pants—even when milking the cows or working in the field.

To Make: Glue this page to poster board. When it dries, color, then cut out the pioneer girl and her clothes.

Dress

Shawl

Bonnet

Apron

Shoes

Pioneer Paper Dolls: Boy (page two)

Country boys like those described in the "Little House" series dressed like little men. Their shirts, pants, and jackets were often patched and repatched. Because belt loops did not become popular until the 1900s, pants were held up with *braces*, or suspenders. Boys often ran barefoot in the summer, which saved on shoes.

To Make: Glue this page to poster board. When it dries, color, then cut out the pioneer boy and his clothes.

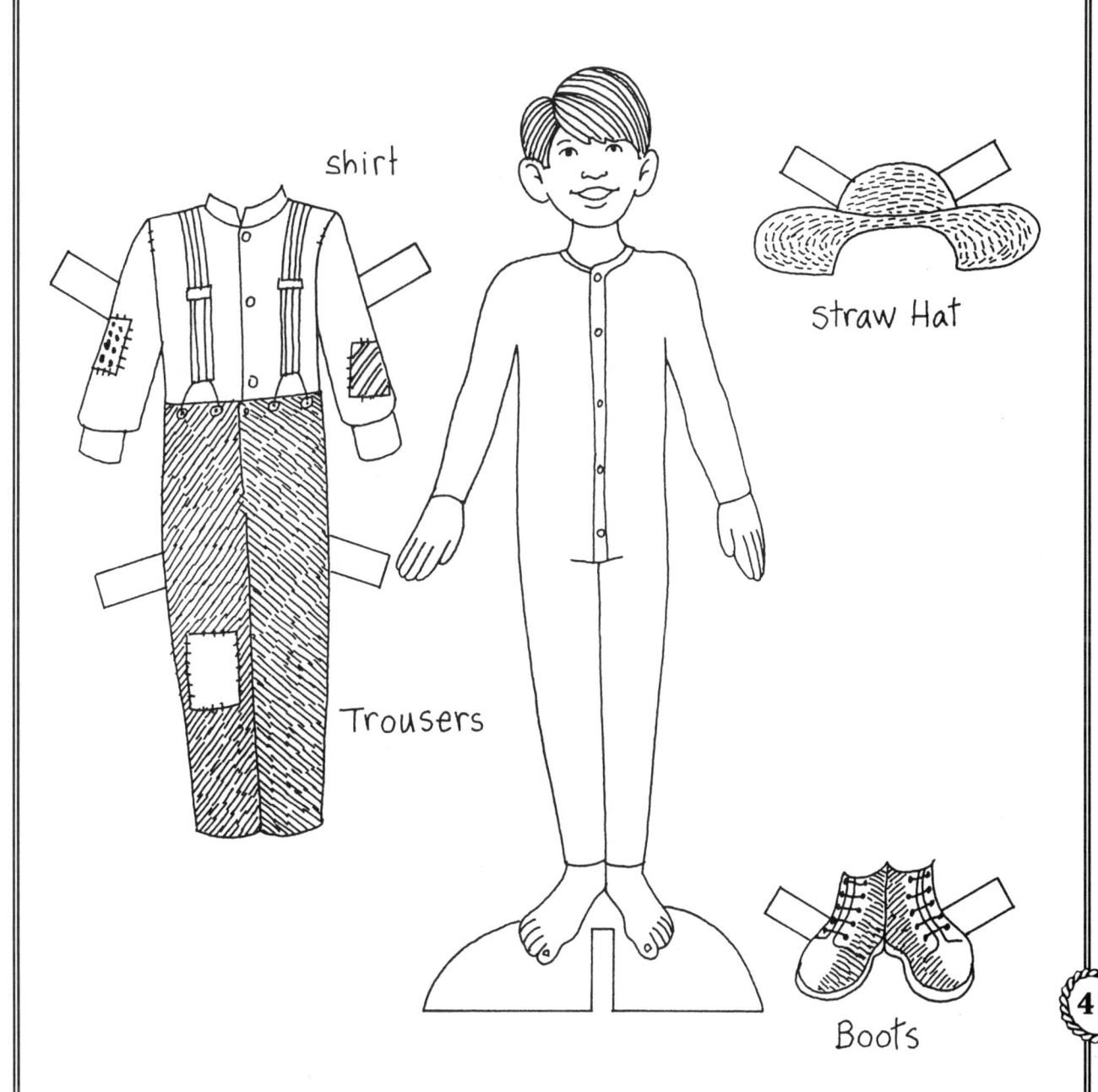

shirt

straw Hat

Trousers

Boots

Pioneer Paper Dolls: Woman (page three)

Country women like Ma wore plain floor-length dresses of calico or gingham. Usually they had only two or three dresses. One of those dresses was saved for special occasions. Country women often wore large sunbonnets to protect their face from the harsh sun.

To Make: Glue this page to poster board. When it dries, color, then cut out the pioneer woman and her clothes.

Bonnet

Dress

Apron

Shoes

Pioneer Paper Dolls: Man (page four)

Farmers like Pa usually wore shirts, pants, and jackets made from coarse, heavy fabrics—most often cotton, canvas, or denim. The Levi Strauss Company introduced a rugged brand of denim pants in the 1850s. Most men held up their pants with suspenders or thick leather belts. All men wore hats.

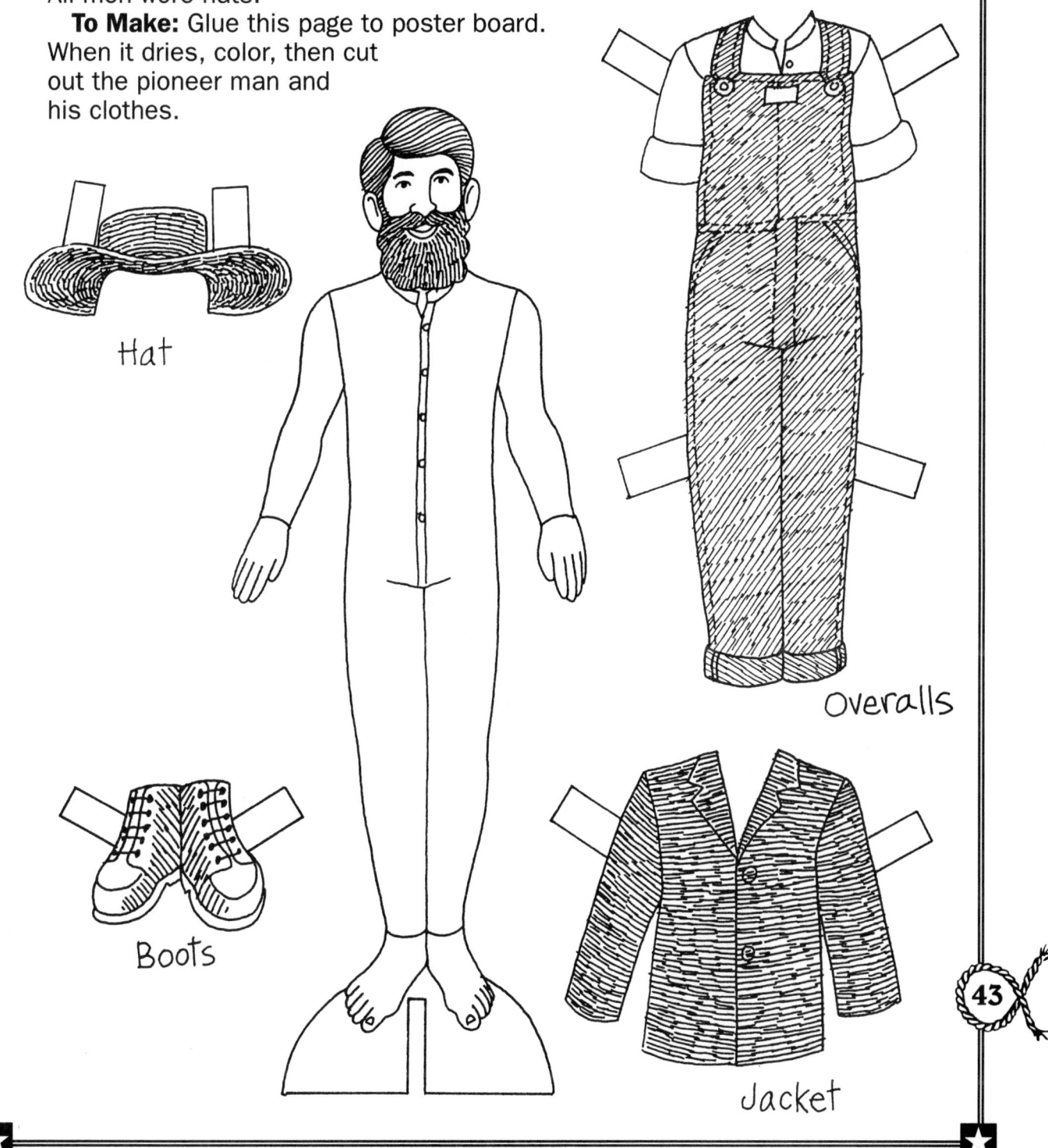

To Make: Glue this page to poster board. When it dries, color, then cut out the pioneer man and his clothes.

Hat

Overalls

Boots

Jacket

43

Community News (page one)

The picture on the left shows a copy of a De Smet newspaper, the *Kingsbury County News*, from 1886. This four-page newspaper kept folks like the Ingalls family informed about what was going on around town. On the right are some announcements from that paper. Read and discuss them with your group.

ANNOUNCEMENTS

G.C. Bradley is running the shelving in his store cellar up to the ceiling to make room for new stock.

Our new barber is a daisy. Just right!

Dirt will soon fly on the train line running northwest, connecting us with Bismark.

Harvey Appleton is such a smiler! It's a baby boy at his house. His name is Grover.

Archer and Howes grain warehouse will soon be finished. Farmers will rejoice over this!

Dr. Kreychie is making immense sales of his horse powders. Well, he ought to, for they are they best powders out.

We almost had a fire at the Northwestern Hotel Thursday morning. One of the girls employed there let a lamp burn and the clothing near it caught fire.

Mrs. Mary Sias commenced a four month term of school in No. 5 Monday.

G.H. Durkee has sold his large team of horses to John Rockwell. Johnny can still be heard to being saying Whoa! Gee haw! without thinking.

Mrs. Cox has sold her homestead two miles east of town, and expects to winter in her old home in Iowa.

Joel Stephens and Etta Cottrell were married, Sept. 17, 1886. May they never know what sorrow is and their pathway be strewn with flowers... Saturday evening "the boys" indulged in serenading the happy couple. They marched forth armed with horns, cowbells, tin pans and various instruments.

Now work with your group to create your own community newspaper on the following page. Here's how:

1. Choose a name for your newspaper.

2. Under the heading "The Scoop!," write a short news story about something important that is happening in your group, school, town, or city. Draw a picture to accompany the article and write a caption for it.

3. Under the heading "Announcements," write one or more announcements about each member of your group.

4. Under the heading "Editorial Staff," sign your names.

5. When you're done, share your newspaper with the rest of the class.

Community News *(page two)*

Name of newspaper

Today's date

THE SCOOP!

caption for picture

ANNOUNCEMENTS

1.

2.

3.

4.

5.

6.

EDITORAL STAFF

Name _____

Buy This!

Here are a few advertisements from an 1886 copy of the *Kingsbury Country News*—a newspaper that Laura and her family read. Take a look at them, then create your own old-fashioned advertisement in the box below. Use the "Little House" books to research some items that you might sell in a pioneer town like De Smet.

Hear Us Twitter!

We have the Largest and Best-Selected Stock of

BOOTS AND SHOES

Dry Goods, Notions, Crockery,

GROCERIES, &C.,

TO BE FOUND IN

Manchester, Dak.

ALWAYS ASK FOR

Bjornson & Keller Bros.,

And Get Your Money's worth.

EUREKA Horse Powders

SOMETHING NEW.

EMINENTLY PRACTICAL AND USEFUL

TO EVERY STOCK OWNER.

The only Horse Powders manufactured according to rational principles, and that can be relied upon for the cure of the various Diseases of Horses and Cattle.

THEY ARE PUT UP AND NUMBERED AS FOLLOWS:

- No. 1—Or Condition Powder is a Tonic and Appetizer.
- No. 2—Is an Alterative or Blood Purifier.
- No. 3—For All Diseases of the Kidneys and Liver.
- No. 4—Is a Worm Powder of unequalled efficacy.
- No. 5—Is for Heaves.
- No. 6—For Coughs, Bronchitis, Influenza, Etc.

ASK FOR DESCRIPTIVE CIRCULARS.

These Powders have been given a thorough and critical trial, and we guarantee them to do what we claim for them.

Manufactured by the Dacota Proprietary Co., Iroquois, Dakota.

Sold by the Leading Druggists in Kingsbury Co

G. C. BRADLEY, De Smet.   C. C. MAXWELL, Arlington.   I. A. KEITH, Lake Preston
DR. J. L. KREYCHIE, Iroquois.

C. S. G. FULLER & BRO.

DE SMET.

Like a large and luxuriant sunflower, the Jackson Wagon comes to the front. Buy it, all ye in need of a good one.

46

READING, WRITING AND 'RITHMETIC

By 1876, nine years after Laura's birth, all states had public elementary school systems, but much of the country still regarded learning anything but basic reading, writing, and arithmetic as unnecessary. Consequently, the average American of the time received only four years of formal education.

School Days

Students between the ages of six and twenty could attend school. A typical school day in 1876 began at 8:00 AM with a prayer, reading from the Bible, and singing a patriotic song. No one sang the national anthem because it had not yet been chosen. There was a national flag, but no Pledge of Allegiance—it wasn't written until about 20 years later! The school day ended between 4:00 and 5:00 PM, with an hour for recess and dinner at noon. Since there was little paper, children learned their subjects through recitation and memorization. Strict discipline was expected from students, and teachers came equipped with a strap or a yardstick to ensure children's obedience to the rules. (Small wonder, then, that in *Little Town on the Prairie*, Laura and her fellow students are shocked by the teacher's easy manner.)

One Room School House

The typical prairie schoolhouse was a one-room building with two or three windows at each long side. A cast-iron stove provided heat; the sun was the sole source of light. The teacher's desk was on a raised platform at one end of the room. Shortly after the Ingalls clan settled in De Smet, the community equipped the school with two-student seats bolted to the floor.

Valued Books

School texts were often among the few books to reach the frontier home. As a result, they were welcomed by parents who, in some cases, learned to read along with their children.

The most important texts were Noah Webster's "blue-back" speller and *William McGuffey's Eclectic Reader*. A number of arithmetic, history, and geography books supplemented these standards. To save money, parents often passed outdated books from one child to the next, so students within a classroom often had many different editions of books, making it harder for the teacher to conduct a lesson.

Student Activities

YOU BE THE TEACHER:

On page 49 is a photograph of the first school that Laura taught in along with some questions to hone students' critical-thinking skills. Distribute photocopies of this page to groups of students, challenging them to work together to solve Laura's classroom quandaries. When everyone's done, invite the groups to share their responses with the class. Be sure you have a copy of *These Happy Golden Years* on hand so that children can learn how Laura handled these situations.

A LESSON FROM LONG AGO:

On page 50 is a lesson from *The National School Primer*, an actual school text used by children in the late 19th century. Students will probably enjoy trying to solve these word-building puzzles. You may want to use the textbook page as a springboard for discussing how schooling in the 1800s differs from schooling today. Share some of the above background information with children and have them look for descriptions of school life in the "Little House" books. Create a class chart comparing and contrasting schools in Laura's day with schools today.

FUN AND GAMES:

School was also a social experience for children of the 19th century. On page 51 are instructions for making and playing a game similar to one children played in the 19th century.

Name(s) _____

You Be the Teacher

Can you imagine being a school teacher at the age of 15? Laura was. This picture shows a replica of the first school that she taught in. The school was twelve miles away from her home in De Smet. It had five students who ranged in age from nine to sixteen. Laura's salary was $20 a month.

Below are some of the dilemmas Laura faced in her classroom. How would you solve these problems? Write your answers on the lines below, then refer to *These Happy Golden Years* to see what Laura did.

1. There was a blizzard last night. Martha and Charles are late to school because they had to break a path through the snow. Should you mark them late? Why? _____

_____

2. Clarence pulls Martha's pigtails because he wants attention. Should you punish him? Why? _____

_____

3. It's 20 degrees in the classroom. The students near the stove are warm enough to concentrate on their lessons, but the other students cannot. What should you do? _____

_____

4. The wind is howling outside because a blizzard is on its way. Should you dismiss school early? Why? _____

_____

5. Tommy and Ruby share one spelling book, but are studying lessons on different pages. Can you think of a way for them to use the book at the same time? _____

_____

49

A Lesson From Long Ago

THE WORD-BUILDER

This picture shows a page from a textbook children used in Laura's day. It was printed in 1868. Look at the way the girl in the picture is building new words by adding just one letter to each line of the puzzle. Then try doing the word-building puzzles below.

Remember: Each line of the puzzle must be a real word. You can add a letter to either the beginning or end of the word. You may want to do the puzzles in pencil, so you can try different letters if you get stuck.

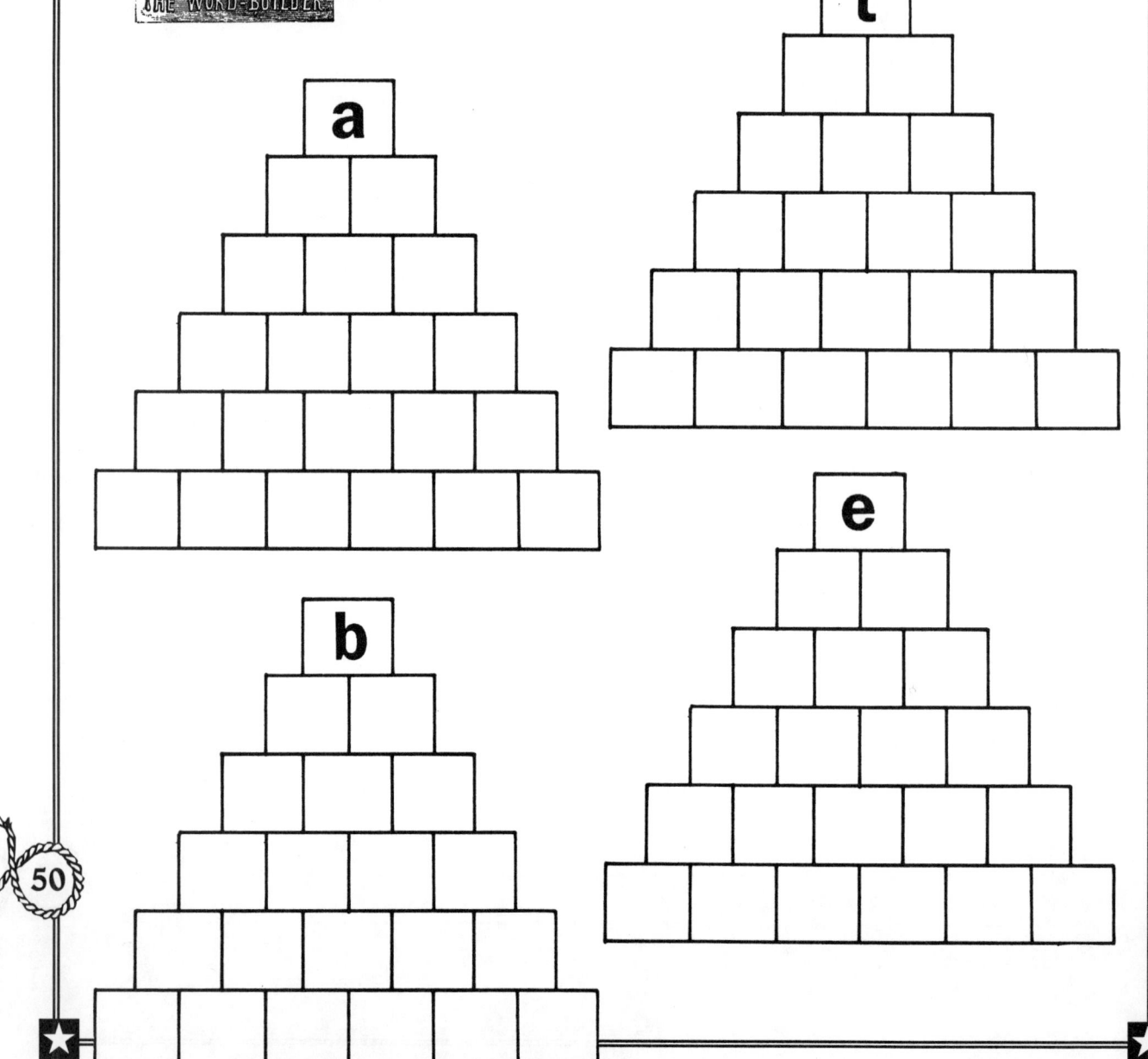

Name _____

Fun and Games

Children in Laura's day played some games that kids still play today, such as Simon says, jacks, and hopscotch. Here's a game children used to play called graces. It's a little like ring toss.

———————— **Materials** ————————
- 2 thin sticks about a 12 inches long (you can use dowels, sticks, or any other material that's handy)
- 2 plastic lids that are the same size (such as coffee can lids)
- scissors
- a pen

To Make the Hoops:

1. Poke the pen point into the middle of each plastic lid.

2. Carefully poke your scissors through the hole you made, and cut out the entire center part of each lid so you end up with two giant rings. These will be your hoops.

To Play the Game:

1. Find a partner. Stand about six feet apart and face each other. (Stand closer together or farther apart to make the game easier or harder.)

2. Hold your sticks crossed, as shown. One of you should now place a hoop over your sticks and then flip your wrists so that the hoop sails toward your partner. Your partner should try to catch the hoop on his or her own crossed sticks.

3. Take turns throwing the hoop back and forth. When you've practiced for a while, try using two hoops at once, throwing the hoops toward each other at the same time.

1. In Laura's day, children played games that relied upon simple, easily found materials—or no materials at all. Why do you think simple games thrived on the frontier? _____
_____

2. What other ways did Laura, her sisters, and their friends have fun in the "Little House" books? _____
_____

WRITING THE LITTLE HOUSE BOOKS

Laura Ingalls Wilder was 65 years old when she began turning the memories of her childhood into books for children. She made many drafts of her stories, and worked closely with an editor: her daughter Rose. A professional writer, Rose helped Laura shape her material into its finished form.

Laura wrote all of her books in pencil on five-cent "Fifty Fifty" note pads. Always thrifty, she wrote from margin to margin. And, fortunately for us, Laura and Rose saved almost every draft of every manuscript, as well as notes and letters. Here's the pad Laura used for *These Happy Golden Years*.

Student Activities

FAMILY PORTRAITS:

Laura's stories focus on home and family. Students may enjoy seeing actual photographs of the Ingalls family, which can be found on the poster in the center of this book. Pull the poster out and display it in your classroom. Then give students copies of page 55, which offers an activity that will get children writing about their own families. You may also wish to share with students that Laura began painting pictures with words in order to help her blind sister Mary "see" the prairie. After Laura described a magnificent Dakota sunset, Mary thanked her, saying, "And now I see it all—you make pictures when you talk, Laura."

Student Activities

BETTER WRITING:

On pages 56-57, you'll find a copy of the beginning of "Making Hay," Laura's first draft of the first chapter of *The Long Winter*. Distribute photocopies of these pages along with copies of *The Long Winter* to groups of students. Have them read aloud Laura's first and final draft (which appears on pages 1-2 of the published book), and compare the two. Students will probably notice that some of the events have shifted place and that the final draft has more details. Ask children to discuss why Laura made some of the changes she did. Then invite each group to work together to complete the two creative writing activities on the second reproducible page.

SPECIAL THINGS:

On page 58, children can see a photograph of Pa Ingalls beloved fiddle and do some creative writing about *their* favorite things. Distribute a photocopy of the page to each student. When children are done writing, invite them to share their descriptions with the class.

SPECIAL PLACES:

On page 59, children can see a photograph of the prairie that Laura adored, and write a descriptive paragraph about it. They are then encouraged to write about *their* favorite places. Distribute a photocopy of the page to each student. When children are done, invite them to share their descriptions with the class.

LIFE STORIES:

On pages 60-61, is a time line highlighting some of the events in Laura's early life, up until the time of her marriage. Laura's stories are slightly fictionalized accounts of these and other childhood experiences. The activity on these pages will help guide children in writing about their own experiences. Distribute photocopies of the pages and have students tape them side by side to show the complete time line. You may want to suggest to children that they ask family members for help creating their time lines if they have difficulty remembering the exact year an event occurred.

LISTENING TO THE PAST:

Children can preserve history by taping interviews with older relatives, friends, or neighbors in the activity suggested on page 62. Invite children to share their finished taped interviews with the class, and then place the tapes in an "Oral History" center in the classroom. In addition, suggest that students transcribe the oral histories and compile them into a big book, complete with illustrations and photographs. Display the big book during Open House.

Name _____

Family Portraits

Laura painted pictures of her family with words. In her books, she helps the reader see each person, inside and out. We see Pa's blue, shining eyes and adventurous spirit. We see Mary's golden curls and goodness, and Ma's quiet smile and gentle manner. We even see Laura herself, with her two long braids and fierce independence.

Use words to create pictures of the people in your family. Write the name of each person under a picture frame. Then write a few sentences that describe that person. Talk about what makes each person special. Don't forget to include yourself!

You can draw more picture frames on the back of this page if you wish.

Name (s) _____

Better Writing (page one)

> *The Hard Winter*
> *Chapter One*
> *Making Hay.*
>
> The whirr of the mowing machine sounded cheerfully from the old buffalo wallow south of the claim shanty. Blue stem grass stood thick and tall there and Pa was cutting it for hay.
>
> Laura brought a pailful of water from the well at the edge of the Big Slough. She rinsed the stone water jug to cool it, then filled it full of the fresh water, corked it tightly and started with it for the hayfield. The sunshine was bright and hot and Pa would be thirsty, for it was only three o'clock of a hot afternoon. There would be hours yet of mowing before Pa would stop work for night.
>
> As Laura carried the jug of water to the field, she watched the clouds of white butterflies hovering over the path and a dragon fly with lovely, gauzy wings chasing a gnat. Laura knew they were dragon-flies because Ma said so, but Pa called them Devil's darning needles and Laura

Here's a page in Laura's own handwriting from the first draft of *The Long Winter*. Compare it with the edited version, which appears on pages 1-2 of the published book. What things have been changed? Discuss them with your group.

List some of the things that you change when editing your own writing:

_____
_____
_____

Name(s) _____

Better Writing *(page two)*

One of the reasons that Laura's stories really come to life is that she relied on all five senses to describe things. Go through *The Long Winter* (or another "Little House" book) and write down a sentence from the book that tells how something:

1. looked _____
_____

2. sounded _____
_____

3. tasted _____
_____

4. smelled _____
_____

5. felt _____
_____

Now use your own senses—and imaginations—to describe a scene from Laura's world, such as her home, school, the general store, or the prairie. Be sure to use all five sense, just as Laura did. (Continue on the back of this paper if you need more room.) When you're done, share your description with the class.

_____
_____
_____
_____
_____
_____
_____
_____
_____
_____

Name _____

Special Things

This is a picture of Pa's fiddle, which was very important to Laura. When Pa played the fiddle, it made Laura feel warm and safe and loved. What object is most important to you? Write about it.

Name _____

Special Places

The prairie was Laura's favorite place—a place she often described in her "Little House" books. Look at the photograph of the prairie. How would you describe it?

_____
_____
_____
_____
_____
_____
_____

Now close your eyes and think of *your* favorite place. Look at the picture in your mind. How would you describe it?

_____
_____
_____
_____
_____
_____
_____
_____

Life Stories *(page 1)*

Laura used her own life as the material for her stories. Paste pages 1 and 2 together to create a time line that shows events that happened during Laura's youth. Do you remember reading about these events in her books?

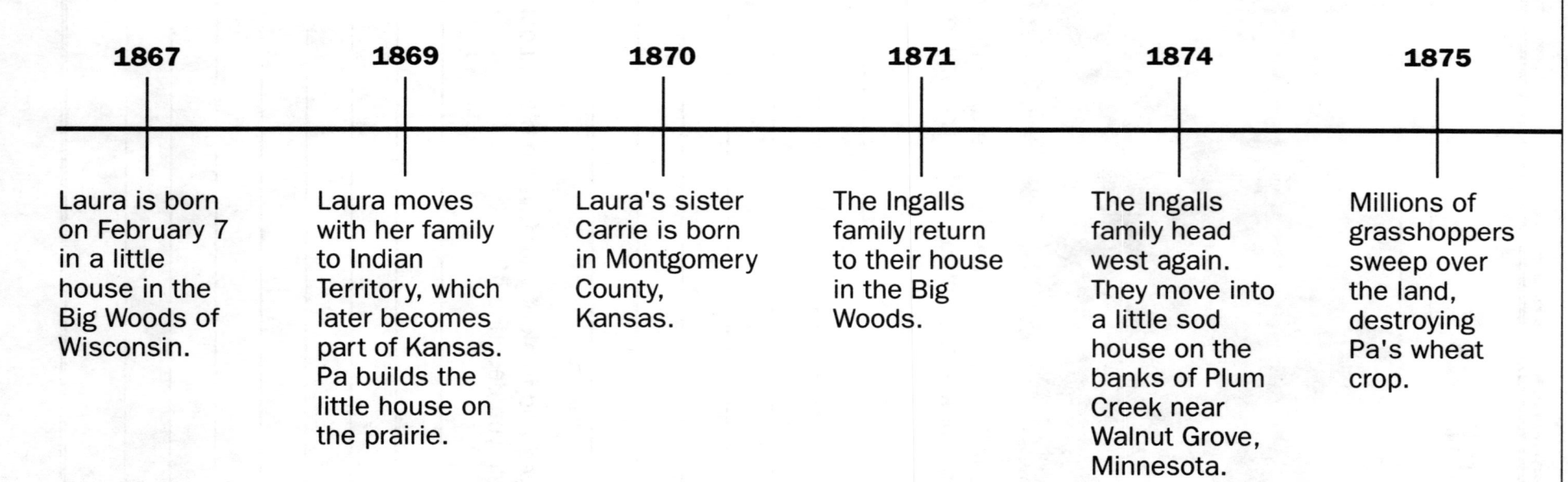

1867	1869	1870	1871	1874	1875
Laura is born on February 7 in a little house in the Big Woods of Wisconsin.	Laura moves with her family to Indian Territory, which later becomes part of Kansas. Pa builds the little house on the prairie.	Laura's sister Carrie is born in Montgomery County, Kansas.	The Ingalls family return to their house in the Big Woods.	The Ingalls family head west again. They move into a little sod house on the banks of Plum Creek near Walnut Grove, Minnesota.	Millions of grasshoppers sweep over the land, destroying Pa's wheat crop.

cut along this line

Life Stories *(page 2)*

Make Your own Time Line: Now make a time line that shows important events that have happened to you and your family. Begin the time line with the year you were born. End it with the current year. You may want to include things such as a special celebration or trip, the birth of a sister or brother, the arrival of a new pet, or a goal you reached (like learning how to ride a bicycle).

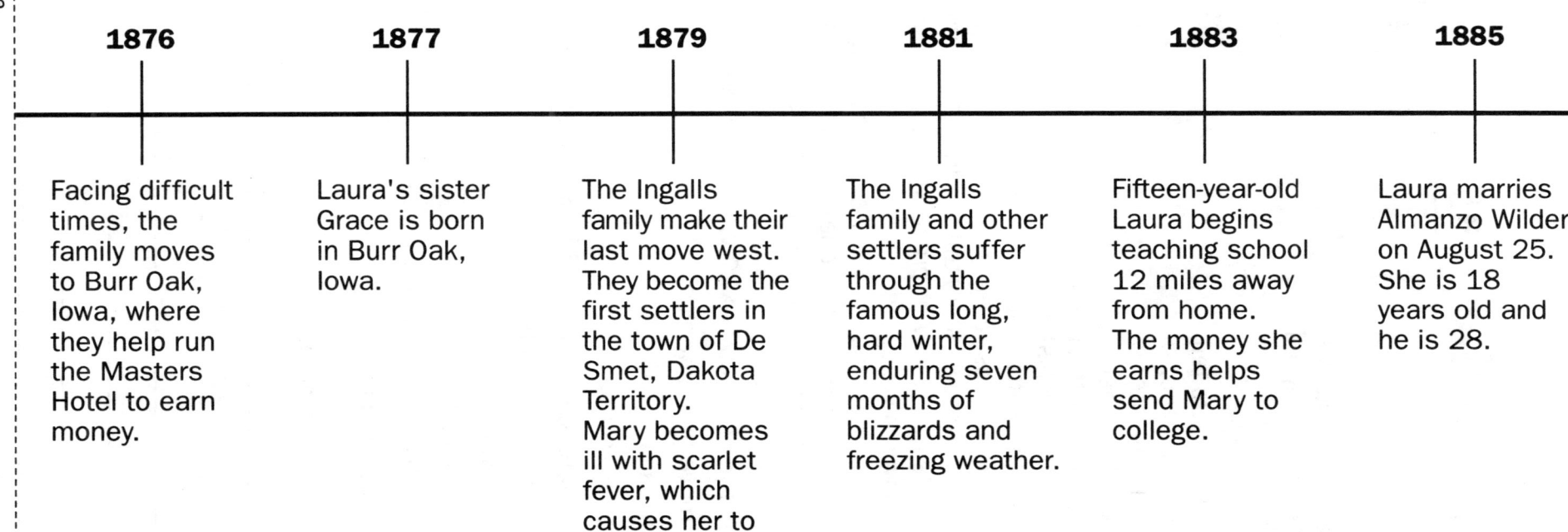

1876	1877	1879	1881	1883	1885
Facing difficult times, the family moves to Burr Oak, Iowa, where they help run the Masters Hotel to earn money.	Laura's sister Grace is born in Burr Oak, Iowa.	The Ingalls family make their last move west. They become the first settlers in the town of De Smet, Dakota Territory. Mary becomes ill with scarlet fever, which causes her to lose her sight.	The Ingalls family and other settlers suffer through the famous long, hard winter, enduring seven months of blizzards and freezing weather.	Fifteen-year-old Laura begins teaching school 12 miles away from home. The money she earns helps send Mary to college.	Laura marries Almanzo Wilder on August 25. She is 18 years old and he is 28.

Write About Your Life: Now pick one thing from your time line. Write about it on another piece of paper. Laura wrote her stories in the third person, which means that instead of using *I* and *me* to tell her stories, she used *she* and *her* and *Laura*. Write your story in the same way, thinking of yourself as a separate character. Use your own name, and *she* and *her*, or *he* and *him*.

Name _____

Listening to the Past

The "Little House" books are a window into the past. They tell us about what life was like in our country a century ago.

Everybody has a story to tell. Ask older relatives, friends, or neighbors to tell you stories from their lives. When people tell stories from their lives to others, they are passing along *oral history*. These stories may never be written down like Laura Ingalls Wilder's; nevertheless, they are handed down from one generation of a family to the next through story-telling. In fact, Laura began writing her "Little House" stories as a way of preserving the stories her father told the family when Laura was a young girl.

If possible, use a tape recorder to record the stories people tell you. Before you begin, make up a list of questions to start the conversation and keep it going. Here are some questions you might ask:

1. Where did you live? Did you like it? Why or why not?
2. Did you ever move to a new place? Tell me about it.
3. What was your family like?
4. Tell me about your school.
5. What holidays were special to you? How did you celebrate these days?
6. What were your favorite foods?
7. What games did you play?
8. Who were your friends?
9. Describe the clothing you wore when you were young.
10. What sports did you play?

Write your own questions here:

_____
_____
_____
_____
_____

Little House Country

If you're interested in retracing Laura's steps across the frontier, or would like further information on her life and writing, here's a list of museums you can contact.

Laura Ingalls Wilder Home-Museum, Missouri

In 1894, Laura and Almanzo moved from De Smet, South Dakota, to Mansfield, Missouri, and settled at Rocky Ridge Farm. Deep in the Ozark Mountains, they built the farm that would be their home until they died. Rocky Ridge Farm is now a museum, and contains the most complete collection of material on the Wilders. Pa's fiddle is here, as well as most of the family's household goods, furniture, and clothing. You'll also find several manuscripts in Laura's own handwriting. The family graves and the Wilder library are nearby.

> Laura Ingalls Wilder Home-Museum
> Rt. 1, Box 24
> Mansfield, MO 65704

Laura Ingalls Wilder Park, Wisconsin

In Pepin, Wisconsin, you'll find a replica of the cabin where Laura was born, the Laura Ingalls Wilder Park, and a museum.

> Laura Ingalls Wilder Memorial Society
> Box 269
> Pepin, WI 54759

Little House on the Prairie, Kansas

Close to Independence, Kansas, is a replica of the Ingalls family's cabin.

> Little House on the Prairie
> Box 110
> Independence, Kansas 67301

Wilder Museum, Minnesota

The Wilder Museum is in Walnut Grove. Two miles away on Plum Creek is the remains of the Wilder home site and dugout.

> Laura Ingalls Wilder Museum
> Box 58
> Walnut Grove, MN 56180

Laura's Home, 1879-1894, South Dakota

Seventeen of the sites mentioned in the "Little House" books are in De Smet, South Dakota, including the Ingalls family's final home and the Surveyor's house. On exhibit are such family mementos as Ma's shawl, a lap-desk, family photos, and Mary's beadwork.

> Laura Ingalls Wilder Memorial Society
> Box 344
> De Smet, SD 57231

Masters Hotel, Burr Oak, Iowa

The Masters Hotel, not included in the "Little House" series, was home to the Ingalls from 1876-1877. It was restored in 1977 and is now a museum.

> Laura Ingalls Wilder Park and Museum
> Box 354
> Burr Oak, IA 52131

RESOURCES

Cassie's Journey: Going West in the 1860's by Harvey Brett, Holiday House, 1988.
How the Settlers Lived by George and Ellen Laycock, David McKay, 1980.
If You Lived with the Sioux Indians by Ann McGovern, Scholastic, 1972.
Indian Chiefs by Russell Freedman, Scholastic, 1987.
Indians of the North American Plains by Virginia Luling, Silver Burdett & Ginn, 1978.
The Indians and the Strangers by Johanna Johnston, Dodd, Mead, & Co., 1972.
Laura Ingalls Wilder: A Biography by William T. Anderson, HarperCollins, 1992.
Laura Ingalls Wilder: Growing Up in the Little House by Patricia Reilly Giff, Puffin Books, 1987.
Laura Ingalls Wilder Country: The People and Places in Laura Ingalls Wilder's Life and Books by William Anderson, HarperCollins, 1990.
The Little House Cookbook: Frontier Foods from Laura Ingalls Wilder's Classic Stories by Barbara M. Walker, Scholastic, 1979.
A Little House Sampler by Laura Ingalls Wilder and Rose Wilder Lane, edited by William T. Anderson, University of Nebraska Press, 1988; HarperCollins, 1988.
The Sioux by Elaine Landan, Franklin Watts, 1989.
The Sioux by Alice Osinski, Children's Press, 1984.
The Story of the Homestead Act by Conrad R. Stein, Children's Press, 1978.
The Story of Laura Ingalls Wilder, Pioneer Girl by Megan Stine, Dell, 1992.

ANSWERS

Tracing the Ingalls Family's Route (page 19)

A Prairie Plat (page 34)
1. Second Street
2. north
3. west
4. Beardsley Hotel

PHOTO CREDITS

Page 34: Roger MacBride/Detriot Public Library
Page 44: William Anderson Collection
Page 46: William Anderson Collection
Page 49: Les Kelly Enterprises
Page 50: Chandler Press
Page 51: Chandler Press
Page 53: William Anderson Collection
Page 56: Roger MacBride/Detroit Public Library
Page 58: Les Kelly Enterprises
Page 59: Les Kelly Enterprises
Poster: Ma and Pa—Laura Ingalls Wilder Memorial Society, De Smet, SD; the Ingalls family—Laura Ingalls Wilder–Rose Lane Museum; Laura and Almanzo—Laura Ingalls Wilder Home Association; Rose—Laura Ingalls Wilder Home Association